Mice

Nocturnal Explorers

Rebecca Rissman

Heinemann
LIBRARY

Chicago, Illinois

Edited by Brynn Baker, Clare Lewis, and Helen Cox Cannons
Designed by Kyle Grenz and Tim Bond
Picture research by Tracy Cummins
Production by Helen McCreath
Originated by Capstone Global Library Ltd
Printed and bound in China by Leo Paper Group

18 17 16 15 14
10 9 8 7 6 5 4 3 2 1

Library of Congress Cataloging-in-Publication Data

ISBN 978-1-4846-0311-6 (hardcover)
ISBN 978-1-4846-0317-8 (paperback)
ISBN 978-1-4846-0329-1 (eBook PDF)

Acknowledgments
We would like to thank the following for permission to reproduce photographs: Alamy: © Arterra Picture Library, 6, 23d, © Chris Lishman, 15, © David Chapman, 10, 18, © Evgeny Drobzhev, 21, © Redmond Durrell, 17, © tbkmedia.de, 22, © TOPICMedia/ L. Lenz, 13, 23e; Ardea: © Werner Curth, 11; FLPA: Derek Middleton, 5, back cover, Gerard Lacz, 16, Hugo Willcox/FN/Minden, 4, Imagebroker, 7 owl, J.-L. Klein & M.-/Biosphoto, 14, 23b, Michael Durham/Minden Pictures, 7 bat; Getty Images: Ivan Bajic, 20; naturepl.com: © Elliott Bignell, 19, 23c, © Philippe Clement, 9, 23a; Shutterstock: Andrew Astbury, 7 fox, Piotr Krzeslak, 7 hedgehog; Superstock: Flirt, front cover, Biosphoto, 12

Every effort has been made to contact copyright holders of material reproduced in this book. Any omissions will be rectified in subsequent printings if notice is given to the publisher.

All the Internet addresses (URLs) given in this book were valid at the time of going to press. However, due to the dynamic nature of the Internet, some addresses may have changed, or sites may have changed or ceased to exist since publication. While the author and publisher regret any inconvenience this may cause readers, no responsibility for any such changes can be accepted by either the author or the publisher.

Contents

What Is a Mouse?

A mouse is a small **mammal** that has a long tail and large ears.

It has short legs with sharp claws.

You might wonder why you rarely see mice during the day.

This is because they are **nocturnal**.

What Does Nocturnal Mean?

Nocturnal animals are awake at night.

Animals that are nocturnal sleep during the day.

Many different animals are nocturnal.

Bats, owls, hedgehogs, and foxes
are nocturnal.

Where Do Mice Live?

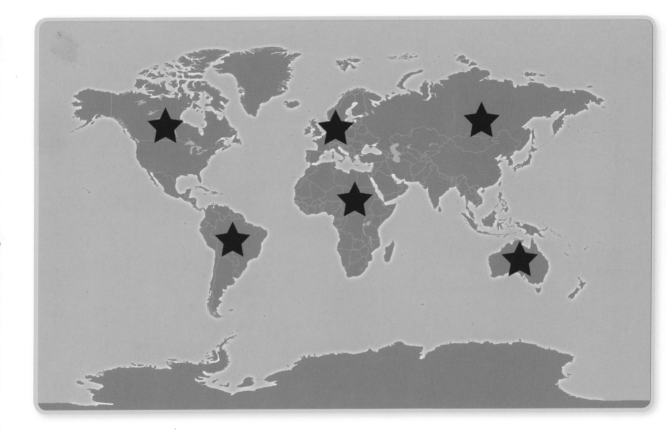

Mice live in almost every country in the world.

They live in forests, fields, gardens, and even in some homes.

Mice dig **burrows** to stay safe and dry.

They make nests inside their burrows with sticks and leaves.

What Do Mice Eat?

Mice eat seeds, berries, nuts, and roots.

They sometimes eat insects too.

Mice living near humans may eat fruits and vegetables in gardens.

They may also eat from garbage cans.

Do Mice Have Predators?

Mice have many **predators**.

Weasels, owls, and foxes hunt mice for food.

Cats hunt mice for food.

Humans trap and kill mice too.

What Are Baby Mice Like?

One to four times a year, female mice give birth to a **litter** of babies.

Mice litters usually have between two and seven babies.

Baby mice are blind and almost hairless.

After about a month, they are big enough to go out on their own.

What Do Mice Do in Winter?

Mice spend time in their nests during winter.

Sometimes many mice share the same nest.

In very cold weather, some mice will move into buildings.

They make nests in quiet corners of homes, barns, and garages.

How Can You Spot Mice?

Mice are most active at night.

Look for small, black mouse droppings. They can tell you where mice have been.

In the dark, listen for soft rustling.

It could be the sound of mice!

How Can You Help Mice?

Do not feed mice. They find plenty of food on their own.

Keep your garbage cans covered. Garbage sometimes makes mice sick.

Do not touch wild mice. They bite!

Mice can carry diseases that make people sick. If you see a mouse, tell an adult.

Mouse Body Map

Picture Glossary

 burrow hole or tunnel dug by an animal

 litter group of baby animals born from the same mother at the same time

 mammal warm-blooded animal that has a backbone, hair or fur, and gives birth to live babies that feed on milk from their mother

 nocturnal awake at night and asleep during the day

 predator animal that hunts other animals for food

Find Out More

Books

Carraway, Rose. *Marvelous Mice.* Pet Corner. New York: Gareth Stevens Pub., 2012.

Morgan, Sally. *Rats and Mice.* Pets Plus. Mankato, Minn.: Smart Apple Media, 2013.

Websites

Learn how to care for pet mice at:
http://aspca.org/pet-care/small-pet-care/mouse-care

Discover more nocturnal animals at:
http://bbc.co.uk/nature/adaptations/Nocturnality

Index